Restrooms 🚻 ↑   Ticketing 🎫 ↗

↑ 🚻 Gates 1-34   Terminals/Parking Ⓐ Ⓑ ↑   Bridge to
🅿 Metro/Parking Ⓒ →

National Airport Terminal

Cesar Pelli

Edited by Oscar Riera Ojeda
Introduction by Paul Goldberger

Rockport Publishers
Gloucester, Massachusetts

SINGLE BUILDING Series: A Process of an Architectural Work

First published in the
United States of America by:
Rockport Publishers, Inc.
33 Commercial Street
Gloucester, Massachusetts 01930-5089
Telephone: (978) 282-9590
Facsimile: (978) 283-2742
www.rockpub.com

ISBN 1-56496-545-7

10 9 8 7 6 5 4 3 2 1

Printed in China

Numbers in bold for each photograph correspond to vantage point numbers on site and floor plans found on the inside front and back cover flaps.

Cover & Front Matter Captions

Cover:	**1**	Vault and drop-off canopy detail
Page 2/3:	**2**	Airside of terminal across Potomac river
Page 4/5:	**3**	View of concourse from ticketing level looking south
Page 7:	**4**	View of terminal with Capitol dome beyond
Page 9:		Final scheme sectional model

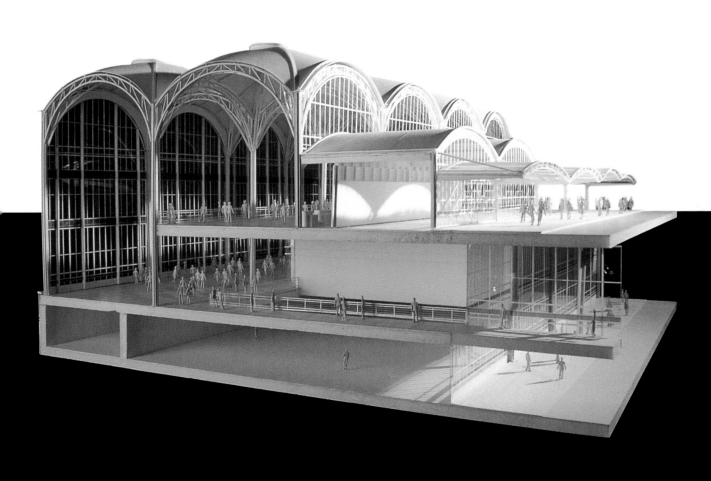

contents

by Paul Goldberger

If there is anything that has characterized Cesar Pelli's career from the beginning, it is the ability to turn the more ambitious architectural sensibilities of a particular moment into buildable realities. Or is it the ability to turn buildable realities into ambitious architectural sensibilities? Either way, Pelli has proven more skillful than most architects in forging a point of intersection between esthetics and the real world, and doing so in a way that feels current but not trendy. His work seeks not to be at the cutting edge of esthetics or theory, but rather at the forefront of the long, complex and convoluted process by which formal innovation moves into the mainstream. From the Pacific Design Center in Los Angeles, completed in the mid-nineteen-seventies, to skyscraper projects such as the World Financial Center in lower Manhattan, Carnegie Hall Tower in midtown, Norwest Center in Minneapolis and the unrealized Miglin-Beitler Tower for Chicago, all of the nineteen-eighties, to a wide range of commercial and institutional buildings of the nineties, Pelli's work has reflected the temper of the times and yet has always possessed enough internal strength to be a product of more than a zeitgeist. He is one of a small group of architects who occupy a position today akin to that held by Skidmore, Owings & Merrill or Eero Saarinen in the nineteen-fifties, straddling the worlds of pragmatism and esthetics, in effect bringing high architectural ambition to the broader public culture. ∎ Whether Pelli is the most pragmatic of high-design architects, or the most design-oriented of pragmatists, would seem to be a semantic distinction, and hardly to matter in the end. But what makes Pelli notable is that he renders that distinction all but irrelevant, since he exists so firmly on both sides of the divide: he is at once a pragmatist and a maker of pure form, and his ability to function on both sides of the line has played no small role in his success. To developers he is

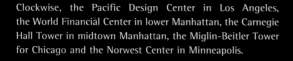

Clockwise, the Pacific Design Center in Los Angeles, the World Financial Center in lower Manhattan, the Carnegie Hall Tower in midtown Manhattan, the Miglin-Beitler Tower for Chicago and the Norwest Center in Minneapolis.

a pragmatist, to architectural historians he is a formalist, and to clients he is both. Thus Pelli seems equally able not only to attract both entrepreneurs and museum directors to his roster of clients, but to work comfortably with all of them. ▌ A sensibility like Pelli's can be useful in the completion of all kinds of projects, but it would seem to be absolutely essential for the design and construction of an airport, a building type that has sent most architects down to defeat over the last half century. Like hospitals, with which they share the problem of a set of programmatic demands daunting both for its quantity and for its inflexibility, airports have generally been designed with the convenience of their operators rather than their end-users in mind. That most airports are technically public, or built by public authorities, has traditionally not made them any more responsive to the needs of the passengers who use them; they are built to be "efficient," and architecture is generally seen as a useless frill, an expense that adds no value. ▌ In the design of the new National Airport terminal in Washington, DC, Pelli was confronted with what was, in effect, a dual challenge. He was required both to solve the programmatic architectural problem at hand and to address the underlying problem of airport design in itself by demonstrating that a more serious architectural solution could be both politically and economically viable. In other words, he had to produce a work of architecture that could compete on the same economic and political turf as less architecturally ambitious airports. Pelli had to use the process that had produced so many bad buildings and bring out of it a good one. ▌ He was helped in this regard by the Metropolitan Washington Airports Authority, a client whose ambitions have always been at least somewhat higher than many other public airport authorities, and which as the custodian of Saarinen's Dulles Airport has had some experience in managing

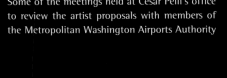

Some of the meetings held at Cesar Pelli's office to review the artist proposals with members of the Metropolitan Washington Airports Authority

airports that aspire to be more than subway stations. The Authority's brief to Pelli placed passenger comfort and convenience equal to efficiency of operation for the airlines, a judgment that seems inherently logical but that in itself represents a reversal of what, for many years, has been common practice in airport design. Only after these two factors did the Authority place its other requirements for the design, that it meet the budget and that it possess sufficient esthetic stature to serve as an appropriate gateway to Washington. Esthetic concerns were presented, therefore, as an essential requirement of the program, if not at the top of the list. It is easy, of course, for clients' programs to be filled with platitudes about the value of design; probably there is no airport in the country that has not been described by its planners as breaking new ground in passenger convenience and pleasure, and these statements often turn out to be meaningless. One of the first signs of the Authority's more serious intentions came early in the project when, as if to underscore the depth of the Authority's commitment both to esthetics in general and to Pelli in particular, the architect was asked to select the thirty artists who would be commissioned to create works for the building, to coordinate all of their work and assure its compatibility with his overall design. ▮ Pelli was asked to develop three schemes in full for the terminal to be presented to the public in 1992. The three schemes eventually became four, as Pelli devised a variation which became the basis of the design that ultimately was built: a building of glass and steel, with prefabricated steel vaults forming 54 modular domes, each roughly 45 feet across. The domes and their interior vaults cover both the building's glass-enclosed main concourse and the parallel entry concourse, where ticketing and check-in is handled. ▮ The terminal is visually light, but grandly monumental: the main

concourse is 65 feet high and nearly 2,000 feet long, awash with natural light, with open views to the airfield for most of its length.

It has a kind of industrialized Gothic quality inside, loosely but not insistently historicizing; as in many of Pelli's skyscrapers,

the architect here has managed to combine the lightness of late Gothic architecture with the tensile quality of twentieth-century

modernism: steel Gothic, but less the heavy, dark Gothic of Viollet-le-Duc than what you would have gotten if Charles Eames had

decided to do a Gothic structure. Maybe the better phrase, given how much this building is pervaded by an aura of nimbleness and

lightness, is Tech Gothic. ▮ The columns and the vaults confer the normal Gothic verticality, which is balanced, in exceptionally

graceful counterpoint, by the predominantly horizontal pattern of the mullions in the glass curtain wall. From outside, in front of the

terminal, the vaults appear as arches, and since the arrival and departure roads cut off the lower sections of the facade, the sense

from the exterior is less of a modernist essay in Gothic than it is of a low, sleek, stretched-out structure, marked by an undulating

line of yellow-painted steel which runs up and down like a sine wave over glass, giving the whole thing an air of plasticity.

The pattern of horizontal glass panels, reflecting a preference Pelli has often shown for horizontal rather than vertical emphasis on

the facades of buildings other than skyscrapers, reduces the Gothic aura still more, and makes the building seem more like a romantic

exercise in high-tech, punctuated by the campanile of a white metal control tower, itself an almost plastic form. ▮ The yellow color of

the interior (and some of the exterior) steelwork is striking; it is stronger than a canary yellow, softer than a taxicab yellow, and it seems

at first to be trying a little too hard to be endearing. Yellow for an airport? Soft colors for any kind of large-scale civic building?

But the initial sense of sweetness gives way quickly to something stronger; Pelli's in-between color turns out to be oddly likable, and to have a certain staying power. It is quirky, but almost anything in an airport that is quirky is to be welcomed, given how much the very notion of fear of eccentricity has governed the design of this building type for so long. The color softens the building's industrial quality without denying it, and it serves as a useful counterpoint to the crispness of the vast expanses of glass and also to the hard-edged terrazzo of the floor, which is black to connect visually to the floor of the original National Airport terminal. If this is not the normal palette for a public building, this seems increasingly to be a strength, not a weakness. ▮ Pelli's most significant achievement—or at least where he managed most effectively to break from the stifling conventions of airport design—is not in color or even in the making of space, but in the plan and section he created for the terminal. Unlike virtually every other airport, in which the airlines' ticket counters fill the wall opposite the main entrance and constitute the largest, not to say the only, visual image the visitor sees upon arrival, Pelli has placed the counters at National against the front wall of the terminal building, so that they are behind the entering visitor. The vista upon entering is not of counters and airlines' logos, but of light, glass and a view to the airfield, with Washington and the dome of the Capitol beyond. ▮ Not the least of the virtues of this arrangement, which was resisted initially by the airlines, is that by opening up the rear wall of the terminal building to light and views and putting the ticket counters on the opposite wall, airline employees who spend the day behind the counter are permitted to partake of the views themselves. The arrival and ticketing level is, in effect, a balcony overlooking the main concourse, which is one level down. Passengers arriving

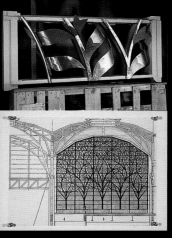

Joyce Kozloff reviewing her design with the mosaic artisans at her studio (opposite page top left) Balustrade and medallion proposals on review at Cesar Pelli's office (opposite page bottom left) Richard Anuszkiewicz's mosaic at the artisan's shop in Italy (opposite page top right) Marble/glass mosaic study samples (opposite page bottom right) Nancy Graves meeting with the mosaic artisans at her studio in New York (left) Drawings and early mock-up of Kent Bloomer's aluminum trellis sculpture (right)

by the Washington Metro system, however, enter through a connection directly on the concourse level, giving patrons of public transit, at least symbolically, an even closer tie to the terminal's main civic space and its arrival and departure gates than passengers arriving by car have. ▌ All passengers, whether arriving by car and taxi on the ticketing level or by metro on the concourse level, eventually pass through the main concourse, which is both the major monumental civic space, the main circulation space and the primary retail area. It bears the rather overreaching name of National Hall, which is a lot for a space that is, at least in part, a shopping concourse. Yet the retail component of this airport, while prevalent, never seems to overpower Pelli's architecture; the space always possesses some degree of dignity. There are stores tucked in everywhere, but they serve at least to assure that the major space will function something like a street, and not be admired and empty. (Criticism of the extent to which the current model for airport design depends upon a high volume of retail stores seems to come mainly from people who do not spend time in airports, where shopping is often the most tolerable way to pass hours of enforced waiting.) ▌ The use of black terrazzo on the floor adds a certain degree of sobriety, if not physical comfort, to the building, and it is handsome enough so that, visually at least, one does not miss carpeting. The floor is interrupted from time to time by a series of ten remarkable medallions, each eighteen feet in diameter, designed by artists who were invited by Pelli to participate in the terminal's art program, including Frank Stella, Nancy Graves, Sol LeWitt, Michele Oka Doner, and Joyce Kozloff. The art program also includes, among other pieces, an aluminum, steel and wood trellis by Kent Bloomer that has been placed over the glass curtain wall at one end of the ticketing level concourse, serving as both sunscreen

and decoration; balustrade panels of porcelained steel by Vincent Longo and Caio Fonseca as well as panels by Siah Armajani composed of steel, cast bronze and copper; a laminated and etched glass frieze by Al Held; a painted-glass frieze by Jennifer Bartlett and a painted sheet-metal mural by Tony Berlant. They are uneven in quality, but even the weakest is stronger than the average art piece added to a contemporary public building, and the level of integration with Pelli's overall design is consistently impressive. Indeed, the National Airport art could not be more different from the sculptures and murals plopped into most new airports, pieces that are intended to distract the eye from mediocre architecture and end up only adding to the sense of confused visual clutter. In some ways National Airport represents as serious an attempt to integrate a diverse portfolio of commissioned works of art with a new work of architecture as any since the art program at Rockefeller Center, completed more than sixty years before. ▮ At this point Pelli's most significant contribution to airport planning has been made; the airplane gates themselves are reached through three piers which, following a conventional, even traditional model, project out in parallel lines from the main mass of the terminal. The gate areas are less notable from the planning standpoint than as a deft piece of detailing, echoing the details of the main concourse and arrival areas in smaller scale. The detailing itself is heavily dependent on stainless steel, often perforated, with barrel vaults creating at least some sense of spatial grandeur; there are particularly handsome stainless steel boxes encasing television information monitors—the latter a notable case of Pelli and the Airports Authority succeeding again in convincing the airlines, which are so often a reactionary force in airport design, to abandon not only their conservatism, but in this case to agree to set aside their individual identities to

accept a uniform gate area design that relates closely to the esthetic of the terminal building as a whole. ▮ Very early in his career, when he was a young architect on Eero Saarinen's staff, Pelli worked on one of the few significant airline terminals of the mid-twentieth century—Saarinen's TWA Terminal at Kennedy Airport. TWA, which has now been significantly (and poorly) altered, stands along with Saarinen's own Dulles, Helmut Jahn's United Terminal at Chicago, and Curt W. Fentress's Denver International Airport, on the notably short list of airports in the United States that deserve even passing architectural mention. Pelli, in his first built airport on his own (he designed a competition entry for Kansai in Osaka, which was not realized) has managed to produce a building that unquestionably belongs on this list. Pelli's new National Airport possesses scale, monumentality and civic dignity, all of which are rare enough among airports; rarer still is to see these qualities in combination with finesse, joie de vivre, and clarity. Pelli has spent much of his career uniting opposites, and here he has managed to join civic space to panache, and air travel to the notion of architectural experience.

Paul Goldberger ▮ New York, New York ▮ September 15, 1998

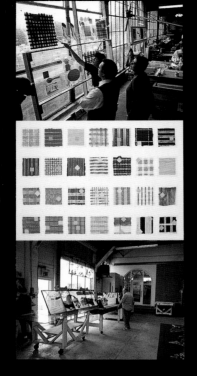

Paul Goldberger is one of the best-known writers in the world in the field of architecture, design and urbanism. Currently architecture critic and staff writer for the *New Yorker*, he was associated with the *New York Times* for 29 years, where he served as architecture critic, cultural news editor, and chief cultural correspondent, and where he was awarded the Pulitzer Prize in 1984. Other awards include the Medal of the American Institute of Architects in 1981, for architectural criticism; the President's Medal of the Municipal Art Society of New York, 1984; the Medal of Honor of the Landmarks Preservation Foundation, 1991; the Roger Starr Journalism Award from the Citizens Housing and Planning Council; and the Award of Merit of the Lotos Club. Mr. Goldberger was named a Literary Lion, the New York Public Library's tribute to distinguished writers, in 1993. In May, 1996, New York City Mayor Rudolph Giuliani presented him with the New York City Landmarks Preservation Commission's Preservation Achievement Award in recognition of the impact of his writing on historic preservation in New York. ▌ Paul Goldberger's books include *The City Observed—New York: An Architectural Guide to Manhattan*, published by Random House/Vintage Books; *The Skyscraper*, published by Alfred A. Knopf; *On the Rise: Architecture and Design in a Post-Modern Age*, published by Times Books and Viking/Penguin, a collection of his articles and essays from the *New York Times; Houses of the Hamptons*, published by Knopf; and *Above New York*, published by Cameron Books.

page middle left) Al Held reviewing glass panels at Architectural Glass Art in Louisville, Kentucky (opposite page bottom left) Glass frieze studies at Jennifer Bartlett's studio (opposite page right) View of airfield from concourse with glass frieze designed by Al Held (right)

Selected Bibliography Terminal B/C at Washington National Airport

Allison, Sue. "The National Airport: Cesar Pelli Talks about the Art in Our New National Treasure." Washington Review (volume XXIII, number 4, December/January 1997-1998): 3-6.

Birchenall, Michael. "New National Prepares for Takeoff." McLean Times (23 July 1997).

"Celebrating National's New Terminal." Washington Flyer (July-August 1997).

Drake, John. "Public Art is the Centerpiece of $450 Million Airport Terminal." Great Falls/McLean/Vienna Sun Gazette (17 July 1997).

Forgey, Benjamin. "Cesar Pelli's Gift: A Capital Gateway." The Washington Post (27 July 1997): G1, G7.

Fortis, Gen. "Architect Pelli: The New Terminal will be a Rich Sequence of Visual Experience." Fairfax Journal (18 July 1997): 6.

Fortis, Gen. "National Airport's New Terminal Reaches World Class for User-Friendly Functions, Aesthetic Beauty." Prince William Journal (18 July 1997): 4, 8.

Guiraldes, Pablo. "El Arte de Volar." Summa+ (v.34 December 1998 – January 1999): 66-79.

Linn, Charles. "Cesar Pelli's new Passenger Terminal at National Airport in Washington DC eases the life of the world-weary traveler." Architectural Record (October 1997): 88-95.

May, Stephen. "Strokes of Genius." Washington Flyer (August 1997): 28-29.

"New Terminal at Washington National Airport." L'Arca (Milan, March 1998): 28-35.

Wiseman, Carter. "Flights and Fancy." ARTnews (June 1997): 116-121.

by Cesar Pelli

The Washington National Airport is situated on a landfill on the southwest side of the Potomac River. From the site there are direct views of the Federal Core and the Mall. The new terminal is located between the existing South Terminal and hangars at the north end of the airport. With 35 gates, the terminal comprises approximately 1,000,000 square feet, including a 1,600-foot concourse designed to accommodate approximately 16 million passengers per year. ▮ The design for the terminal is sympathetic with the context of the historic 1941 South Terminal. As in the existing South Terminal, we placed the functional elements toward the land side and created large expanses of glass to see the federal monuments beyond. Both the new terminal and the historic South Terminal buildings have their own character, appropriate to their time and to the nature of air travel in each period. The complete project makes a coherent architectural ensemble. ▮ Our design is based on a 45-foot-square, repetitive structural steel bay that establishes scale, flexibility and architectural proportions. These spatial, modular units are of a recognizable human scale. Each bay is a dome with a central glass oculus. The dome is one of the most ancient symbols of shelter and also serves to establish a connection with the civic architecture of Washington DC. ▮ There are three levels in the building. Ticket counters and enplane curb for departures are located on the uppermost level; the main concourse is on the middle level; and the lowest level contains baggage claim areas and the arrival curb. From the concourse, the passenger can exit the terminal building and proceed through an enclosed bridge to the Metro, two new parking garages, or to the South Terminal. This design allows most passengers to move efficiently in and out of the building without the need for escalators or

Model showing the relationship of the project with the existing terminal (far left) Domes construction documents (left) Cesar Pelli's office at different stages of the design process (right)

stairs. The concourse is the main "street" of the building. It is an airy, luminous and memorable place. ▮ The Architectural

Enhancement Program (AEP) integrates 30 commissioned artworks in the architecture of the terminal. Each piece is organic

to the building. We decided on the specific locations and dimensions for the artworks only after we had a conceptual design for

the building that allowed us to place and integrate the pieces in the most favorable way. The individual works have been

executed in a great variety of materials: stained glass, marble and glass mosaics, terrazzo, cast bronze, hammered aluminum

and copper, painted steel, porcelain enamel and traditional paint on board and canvas. ▮ We studied many historic and recent

alliances of painters, sculptors, artisans and architects to better understand the potential of collaborations across artistic

disciplines. Programs like Rockefeller Center in New York City and the St. Louis train station were important points of reference

for us and the Metropolitan Washington Airports Authority. We researched the structure and process of other public art programs,

and we considered hundreds of possible artists for the AEP. Numerous local and national organizations were contacted to bring

us in contact with the widest possible variety of artists for the program. ▮ The sites for the artwork include 10 floor medallions

on the main concourse; 11 balustrades that overlook the concourse; five murals; one bridge sculpture; one sunscreen panel on

the south wall of the ticket level lobby; and two stained glass friezes on the air-side concourse curtain wall. ▮ We worked

closely with each of the artists and the artisans throughout the design and fabrication of the artwork. Proposals were

carefully reviewed during the earliest phases of design and these concepts were further explored in models and drawings. ▮

8 9 10 11 12 13 Passanger pick-up (top left) Terminal roof from tower (bottom left) South side outdoor terrace (right) Concourse level (opposite page left) Center pier (opposite page top right) Concourse looking north (opposite page bottom right)

The terminal is a rich sequence of visual experiences. The artwork, natural light, comfortable walking distances for the traveling public and dramatic and uninterrupted views of the airfield make flying through National Airport a delightful experience.

Cesar Pelli ❚ New Haven, Connecticut ❚ September 1997

Cesar Pelli was Dean of the Yale School of Architecture from 1977 to 1984. He established Cesar Pelli & Associates in New Haven, Connecticut in 1977 after a distinguished architectural career that included the design of the Pacific Design Center in Los Angeles and the US Embassy in Tokyo. Mr. Pelli's work has been published and exhibited internationally, with seven books and several whole issues of professional journals dedicated to his designs and theories. ❚ In 1995, the American Institute of Architects (AIA) awarded Cesar Pelli its Gold Medal. In 1991, the AIA selected Mr. Pelli as one of the 10 most influential living American architects. Cesar Pelli has received over 100 awards for design excellence, and he is the only architect to receive a Connecticut State Arts Award.

New Terminal Facts ▮ General Building: ▮ Terminal/connector floor area: 1,040,000 square feet (equal to four city blocks or 24 acres) ▮ Terminal/connector footprint area: 440,000 square feet (10 acres) ▮ Total building length (including connector): 2,225 linear feet ▮ Height of east curtain wall (glass): 54 feet (equal to 1.5 acres of glazed curtain wall, 174,000 square feet of all glazing, four acres all glass) ▮ Number of domes: 54 atop the concourse, 27 atop the pier ends ▮ Upper curb (ticket counter level): 1,600 feet (1,200 linear feet of usable curb) ▮ Lower curb (baggage claim level): 1,470 linear feet of usable curb ▮ Tons of structural steel: 11,000 tons (22 million pounds) ▮ Tons of reinforcing steel: 50 (100,000 pounds) ▮ Composite floor decking: 680,000 square feet ▮ Roof decking: 475,000 square feet ▮ Poured in place terrazzo: 170,000 square feet ▮ Precast terrazzo: 150,000 square feet ▮ Hydraulic elevators: 32 ▮ Escalators: 26 ▮ Moving walkways: 6 (1,100 total linear feet) ▮ Bag claim devices: 12 with 1,760 total linear feet of presentation (area visible to the public) ▮ **Site/Road/Apron:** ▮ Sitework mass excavation: 280,000 cubic yards (7.5 million cubic feet, equal to 1 billion pounds of earth removed)

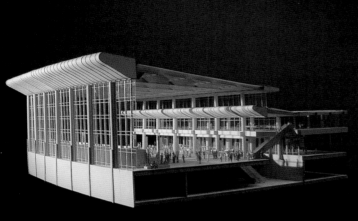

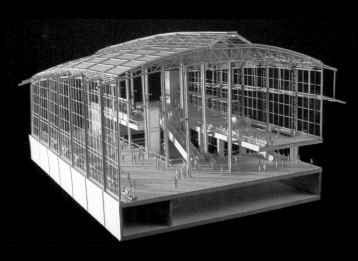

14 East elevation detail (previous spread) Early models and color perspectives, including a variation which eventually became the basis of the design that ultimately was built (above and right) Cesar Pelli's oil craypas and ink elevation sketches (following spread) Final scheme concourse color perspectives (following foldouts)

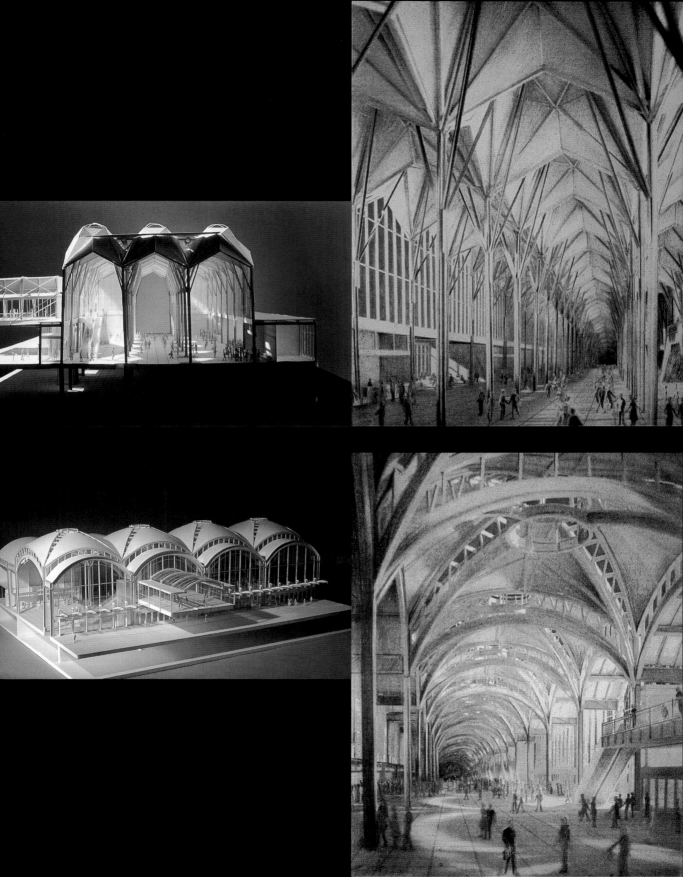

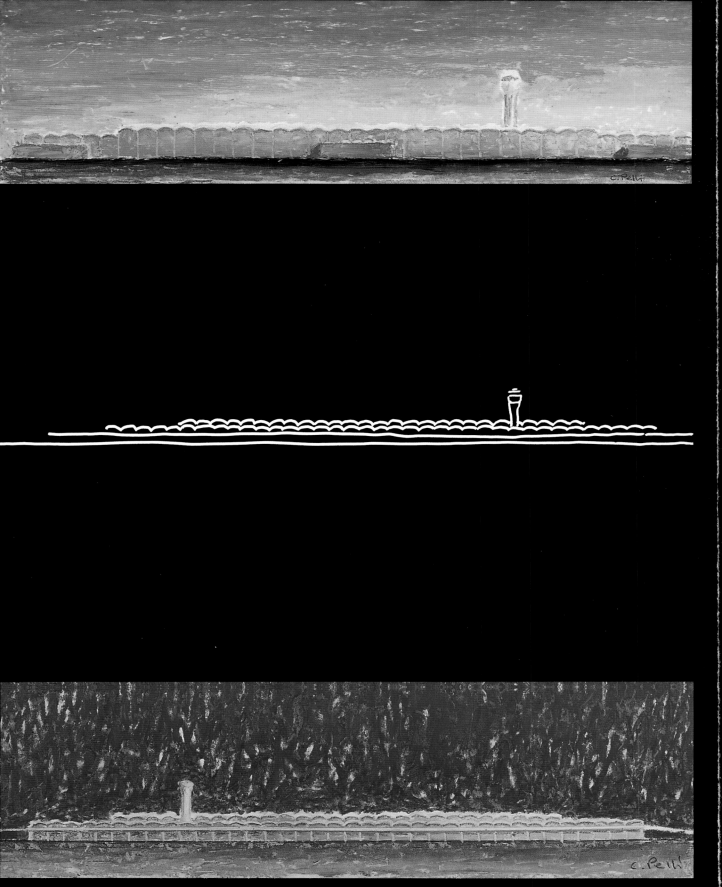

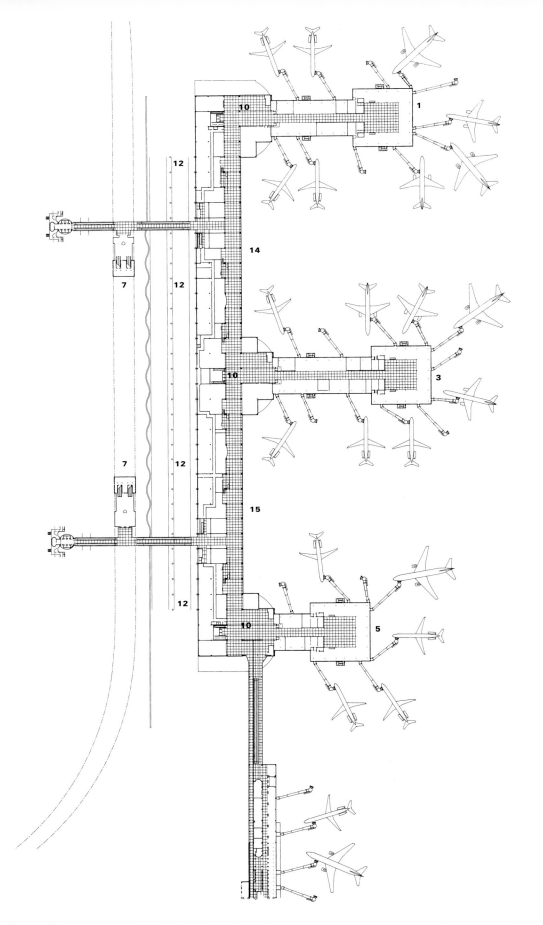

Concourse plan

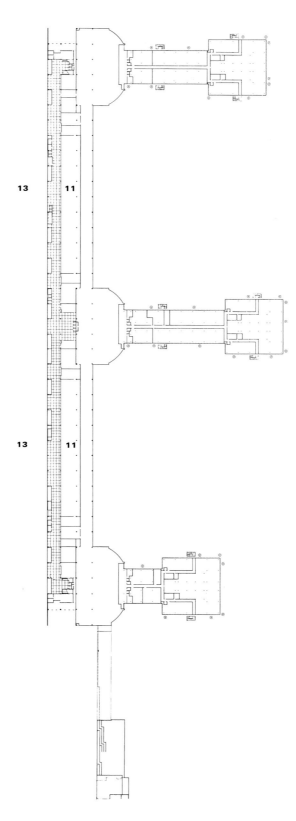

13   **11**

13   **11**

Baggage level plan

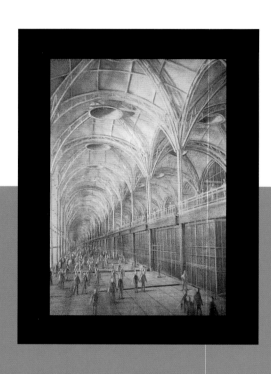

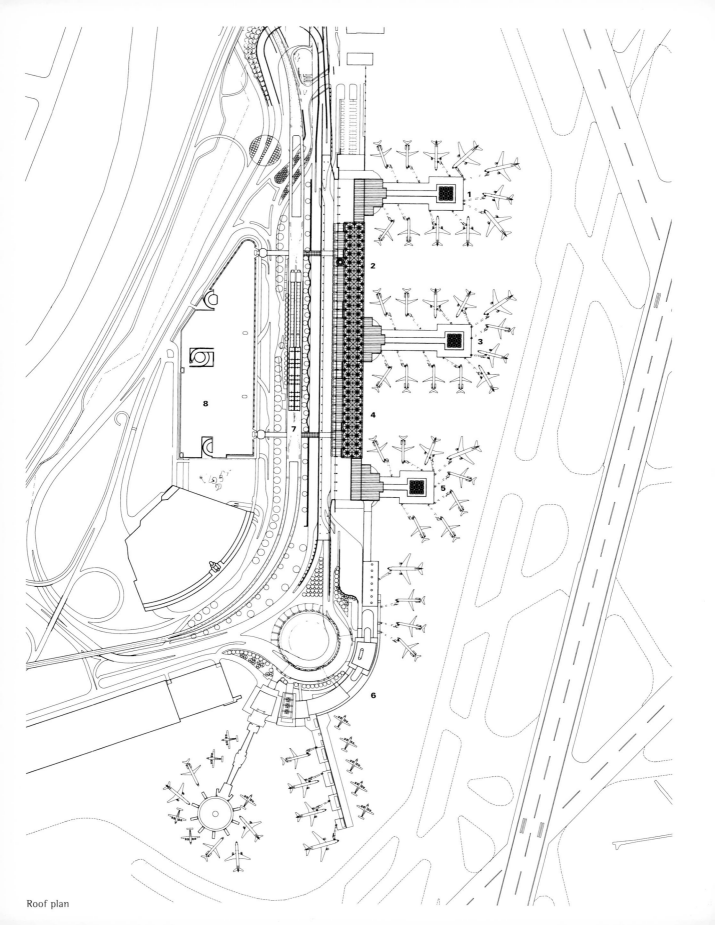

Roof plan

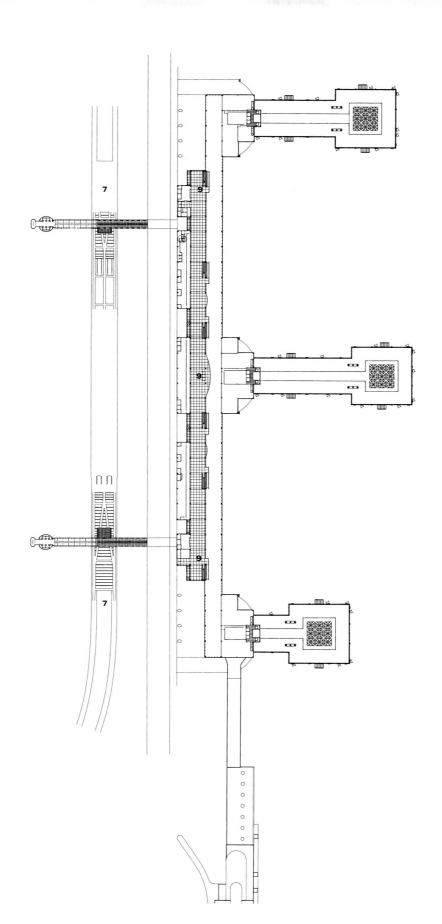

Ticket level plan

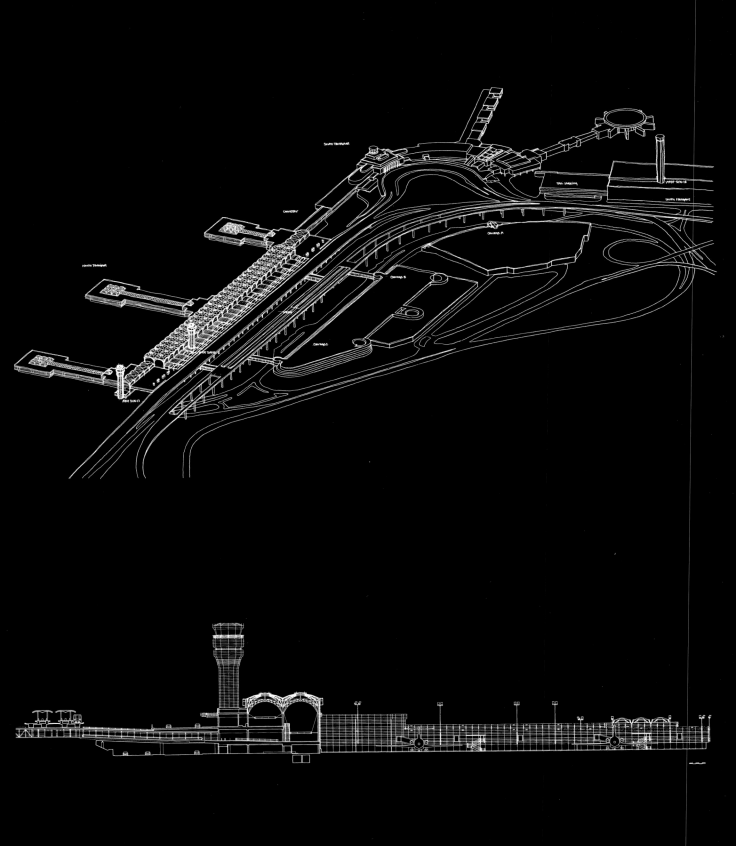

Axonometric: North Terminal, South Terminal, metro station and garages A, B, C (top) East-west section through concourses (bottom)

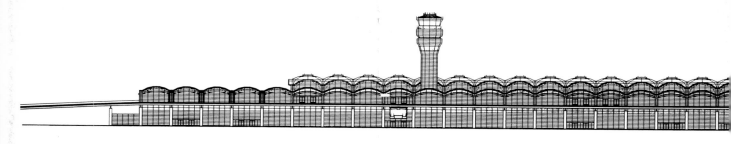

West elevation

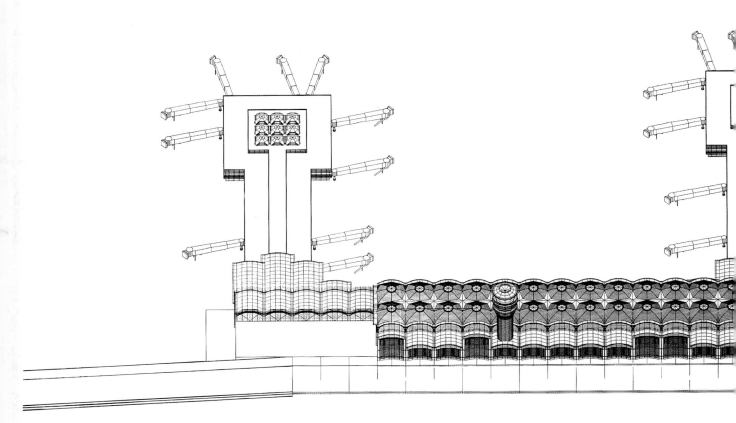

Axonometric

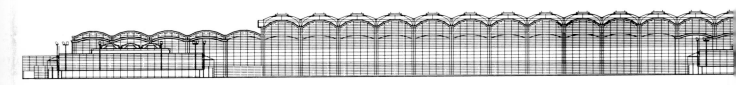

East elevation

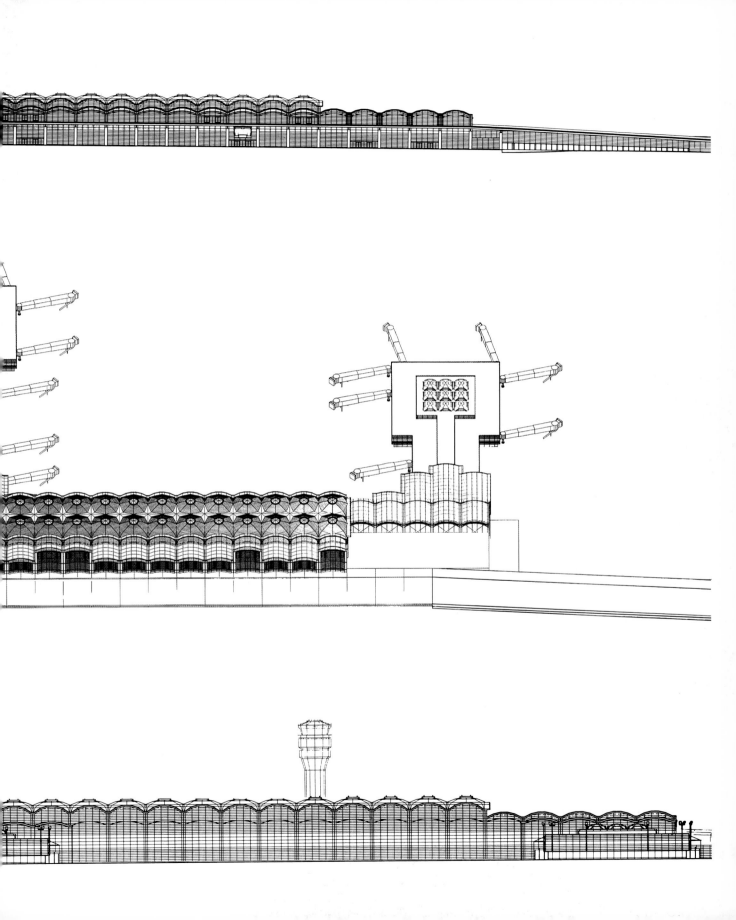

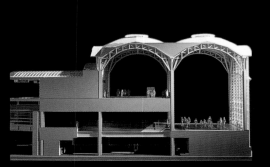

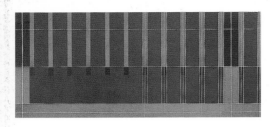

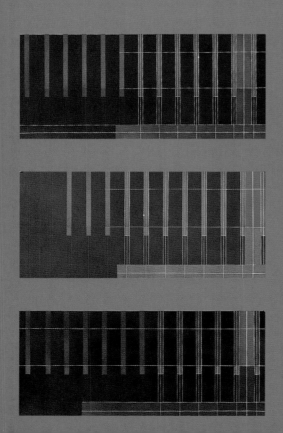

Structural bay and sectional study models (previous spread) Floor pattern variations (left)

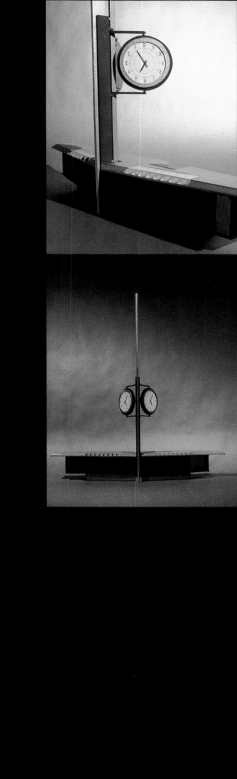

domes structural studies (following spread left). Structural bays and sectional study models (following spread right).

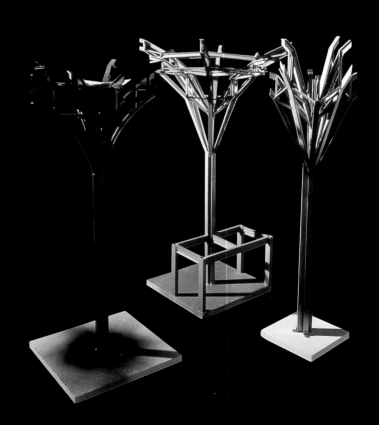

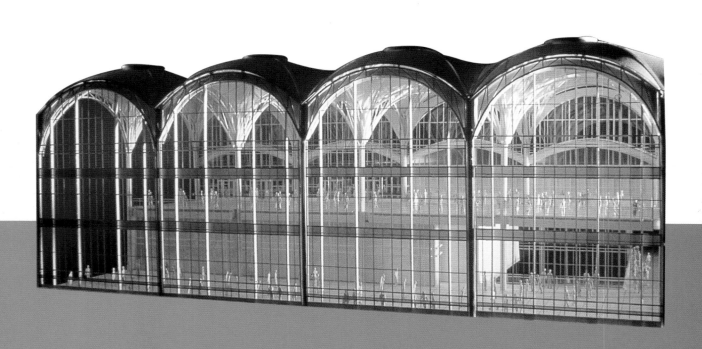

Terminal and atrium model views (previous spread)
Night view: north terminal and control tower from tarmac
(right) Night view: enplane roadway (upper left) Night
view: (ca 1950) of 1941 south terminal (lower left)

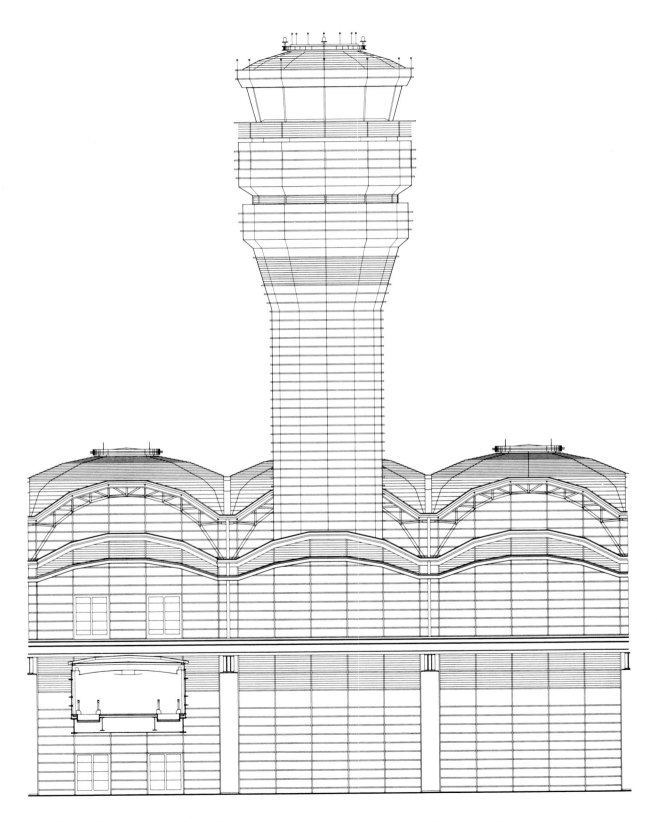

Air traffic control tower elevation (above) Construction process (previous spread, right, and following spread)

1 Joyce Kozloff
2 Richard Anuszkiewicz
3 Joyce Scott
4 Michele Oka Doner
5 Frank Stella
6 Sol LeWitt
7 Nancy Graves
8 Valerie Jaudon
9 Jacob Kainen
10 Gregory Henry
11 David Row
12 Tony Berlant
13 Sam Gilliam
14 William Jacklin
15 Lisa Scheer
16 Edith Kuhnle
17 Vincent Longo
18 Robert Reed
19 Cary Smith
20 Robert Cottingham
21 Wayne Edson Bryan
22 Yoshishige Furukawa
23 Caio Fonseca
24 Eglon Daley
25 WC Richardson
26 Siah Armajani
27 Robert Vickery
28 Kent Bloomer
29 Al Held
30 Jennifer Bartlett

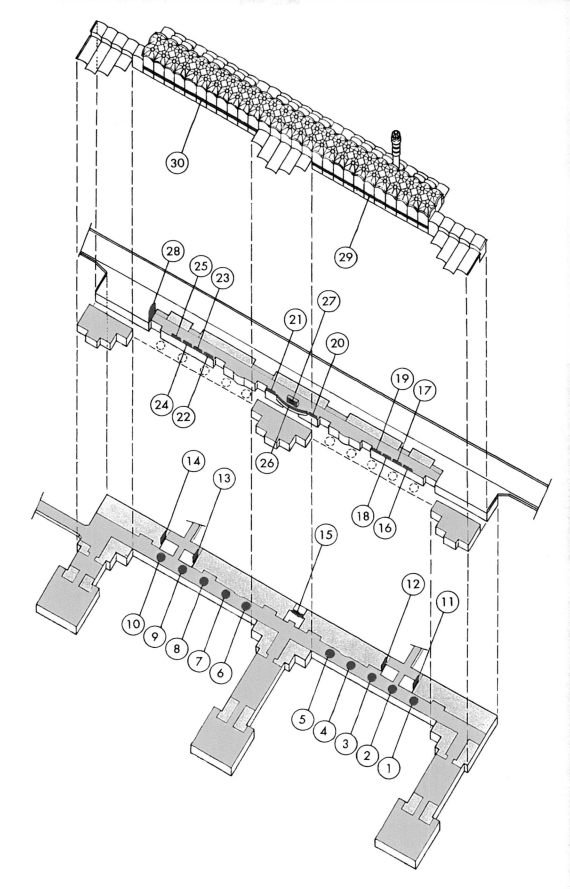

Architectural Enhancement Program, artist location diagram (above) Fabrication and installation photographs (left)

15 16 17 18 19 Terminal view from southeast (previous spread) East facade detail (left) East view (above) Dome detail from tower (bottom) East facade (following spread)

20 21 22 Terminal view from northeast (previous spread) East facade detail (previous foldout) Night view (this spread)

27 28 29 30 Night view from northwest (previous spread) Partial west facade (top) Northwest view (bottom) Metro platform connection to terminal (right)

31 32 33 Southwest views with the Capitol and the Washington Monument in the background (previous spread, left and above)

34 35 36 View from southwest (previous spread) Transverse section through concourses (above) Passenger pick-up (above left) and drop-off (right)

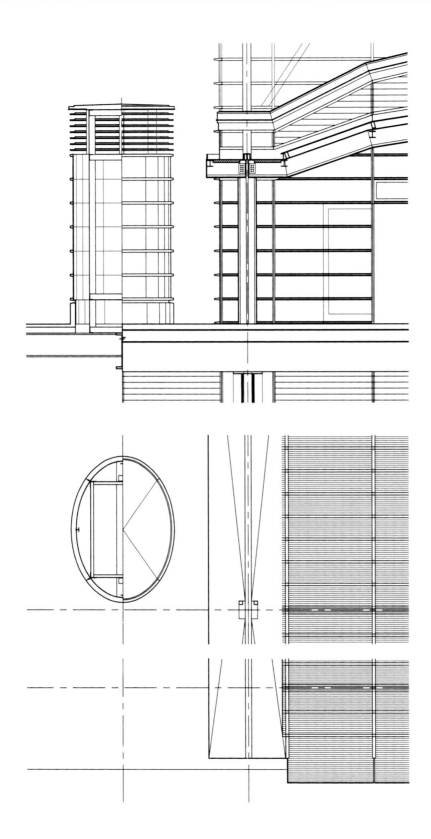

37 38 39 40 41 42 43 44 45 46 47 West canopy detail (previous spread) Drop-off curb looking north (right) Detail of air intake and drop-off canopy (above) Tower views from northeast, west and southwest (next spread, first column, top to bottom) Outdoor terrace from north (second column, top and center) and south (second column, bottom) Drop-off canopy (third column top and bottom) and airside facade detail (third column center)

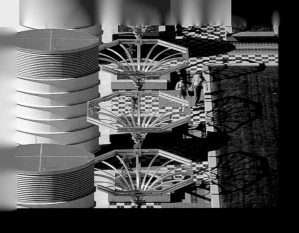

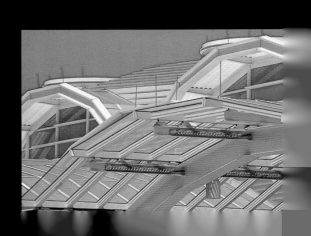

48 49 50 51 North outdoor terrace, looking south (left) North outdoor terrace from north end of concourse (top) and from air traffic control tower (middle) South outdoor terrace looking north (bottom)

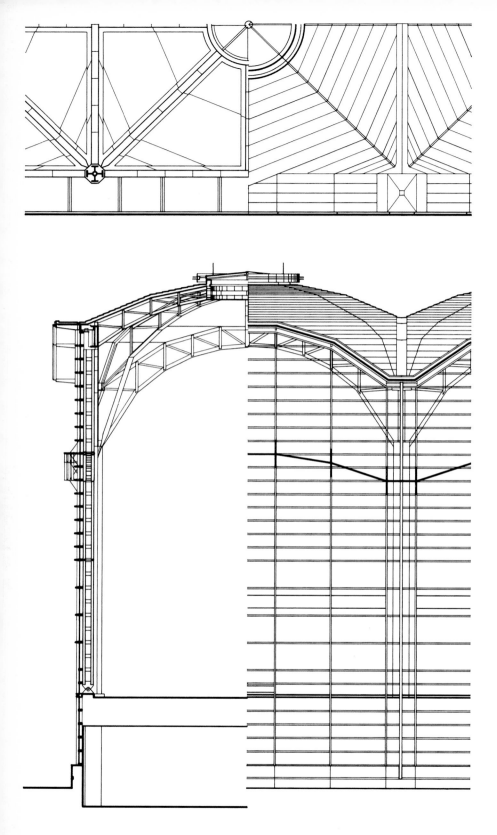

52 53 54 55 56 57 58 59 60 61 62 Ticketing level looking south (previous spread) View of concourse level from ticketing level looking north (right) North terminal structural bay: reflected ceiling plan, roof plan, section, elevation (above) Structural bays and domes interior details (following spread from top to bottom left to right)

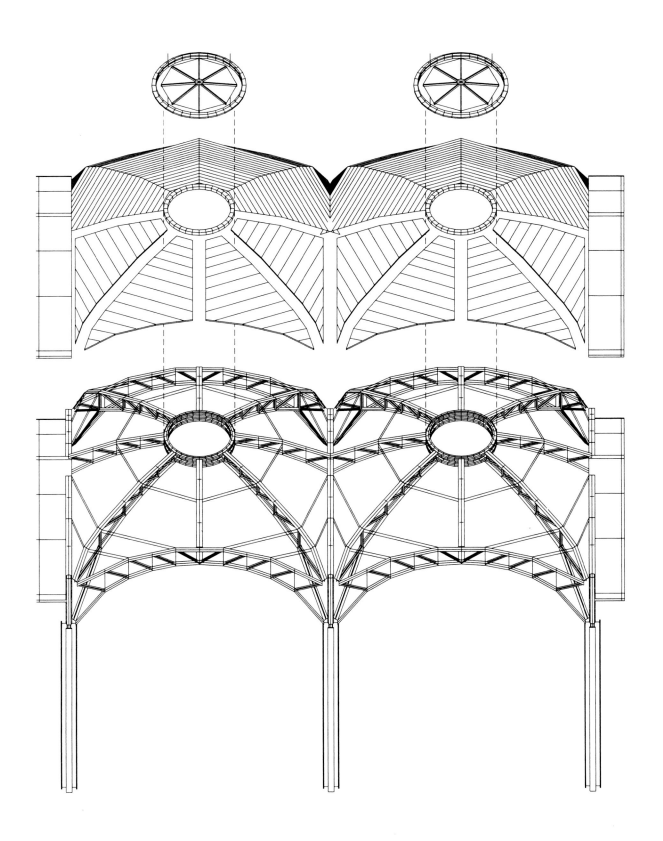

63 Concourse level looking south (left) Exploded axonometric: north terminal structural bays (above)

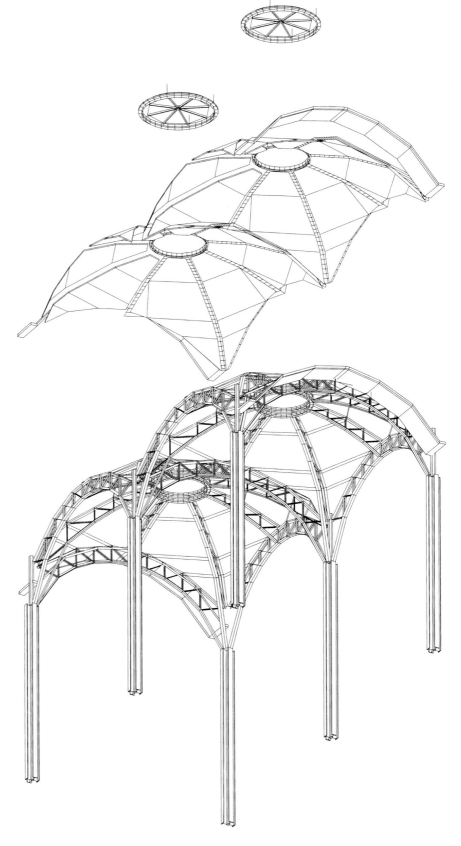

Concourse level looking south (top left and opposite page) Exploded axonometric: north terminal structural bays (above) Passenger arrivals and departures through different concourse levels (following spread from top to bottom left to right)

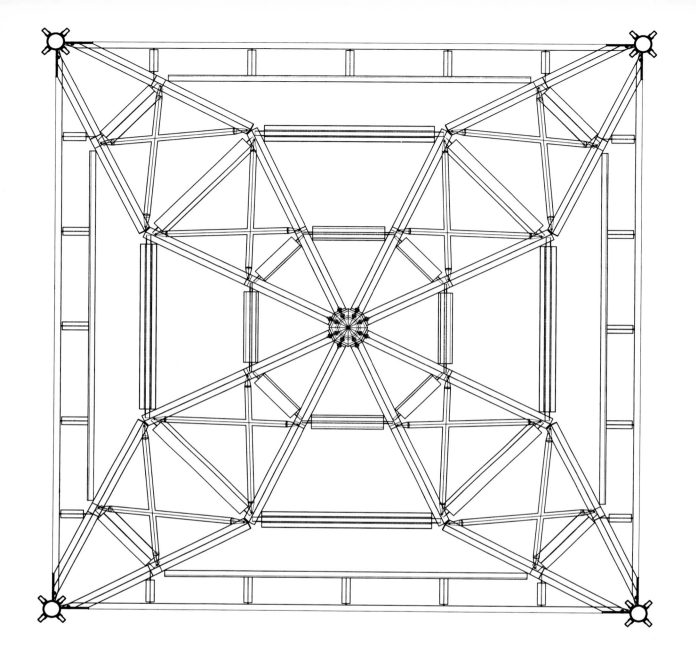

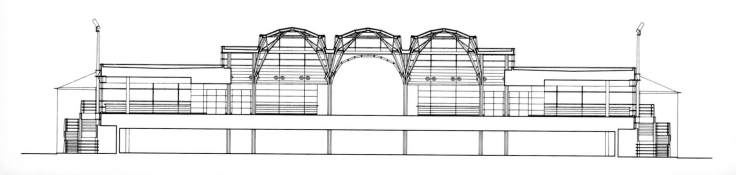

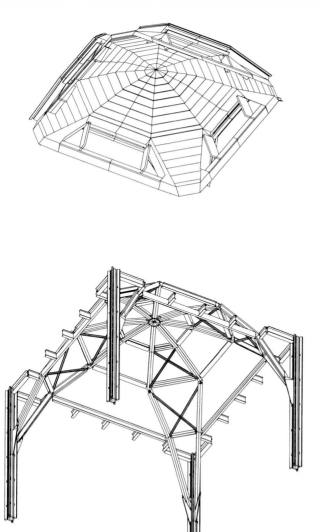

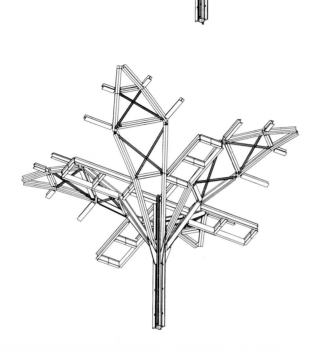

78 79 Concourse level looking north (previous spread)
Center pier (above) Structure in pier domes (opposite page top)
Pier section (opposite page bottom) Exploded axonometric:
pier structural bay (left)

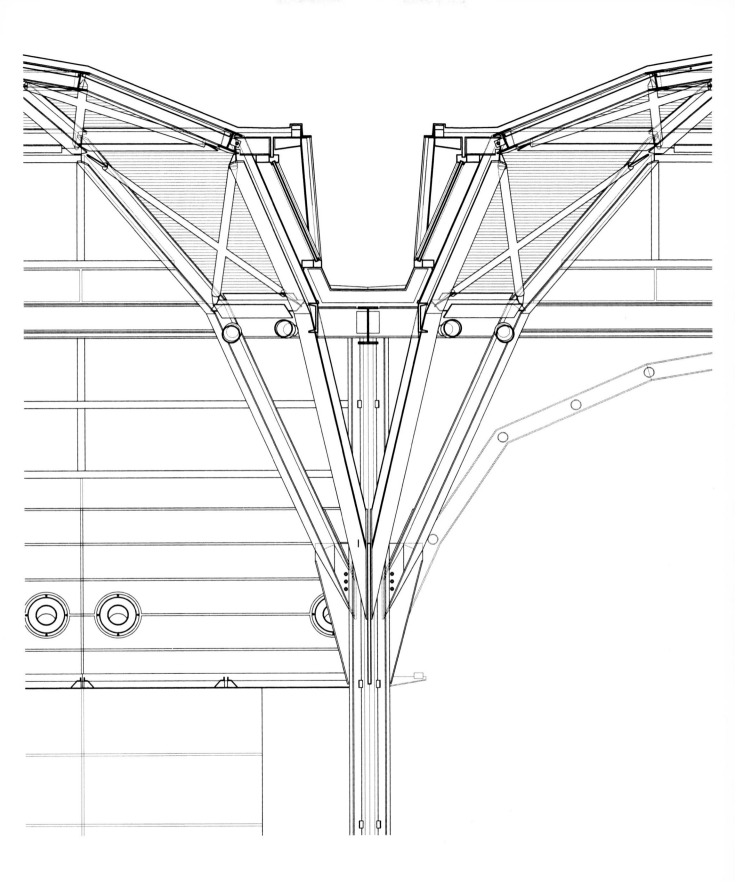

80 Center pier (left) Section detail: Pier roof structure (above)

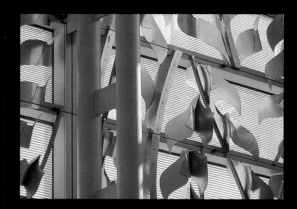

81 82 83 84 85 86 87 88 89 90 91 92 93 94 Details and general view of aluminum, steel and wood trellis designed by Kent Bloomer at ticket level looking south (above, right and following spread first column top to bottom) Al Held glass frieze detail and reflections (following spread second column) Joyce Scott, Richard Anuszkiewicz and Gregory Henry marble/glass mosaics (following spread third column) David Row aluminum panel mural; Lisa Scheer copper, aluminum and wood sculpture and Siah Armajani steel, cast bronze and copper balustrade (following spread fourth column)

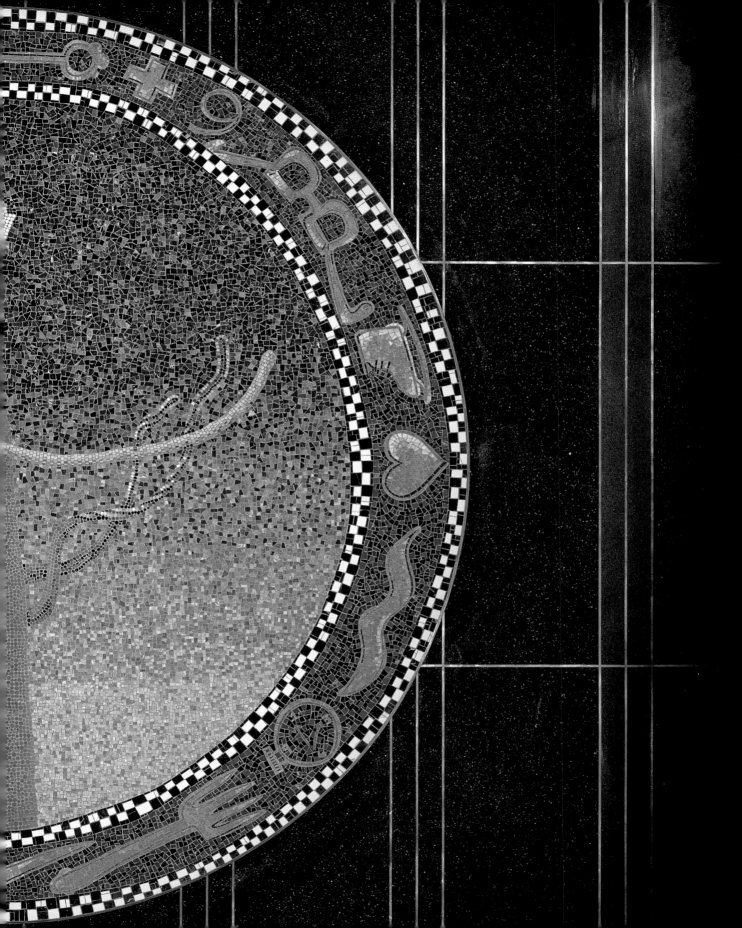

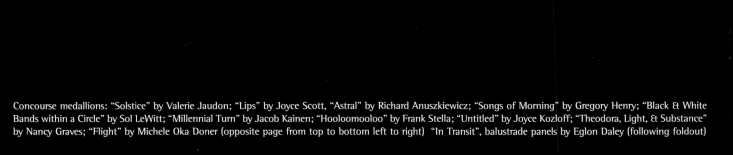
Concourse medallions: "Solstice" by Valerie Jaudon; "Lips" by Joyce Scott, "Astral" by Richard Anuszkiewicz; "Songs of Morning" by Gregory Henry; "Black & White Bands within a Circle" by Sol LeWitt; "Millennial Turn" by Jacob Kainen; "Hooloomooloo" by Frank Stella; "Untitled" by Joyce Kozloff; "Theodora, Light, & Substance" by Nancy Graves; "Flight" by Michele Oka Doner (opposite page from top to bottom left to right) "In Transit", balustrade panels by Eglon Daley (following foldout)

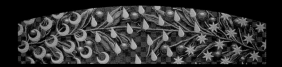

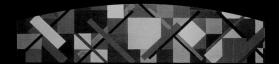

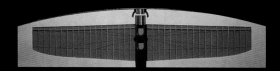

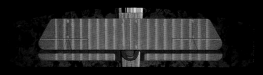

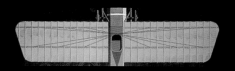

Balustrade panels, from left to right top to bottom: "Untitled" by Robert Reed (1,2,3); "Three-Part Invention" by Caio Fonseca (4,5,6); "Times Roll" by W. C. Richardson (7,8,15,16); "Untitled" by Wayne Edson Bryan (9,10,11); "Municiplex" by Vincent Longo (12,13,14); "Night River Series" by Edith Kuhnle

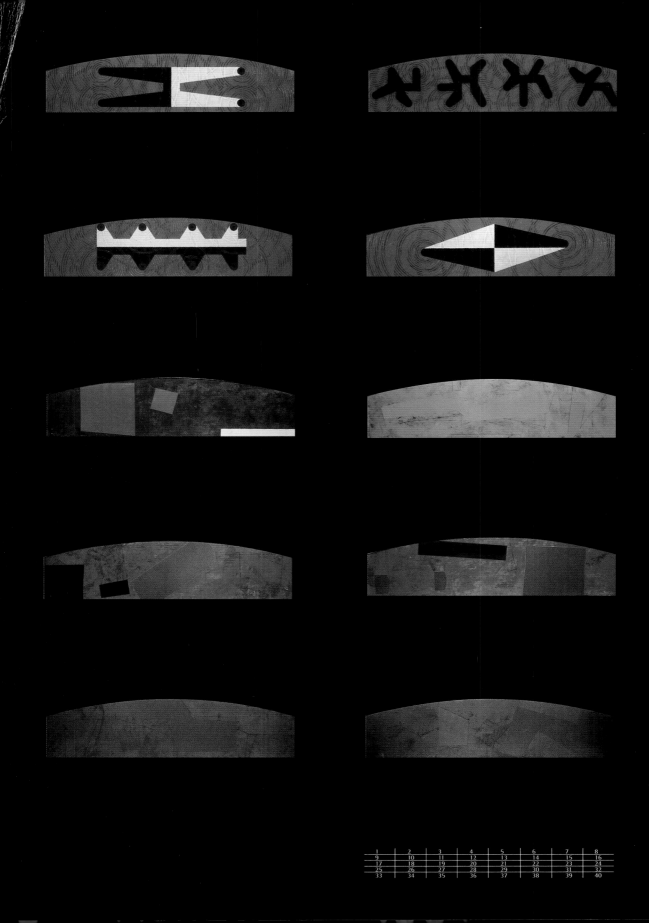

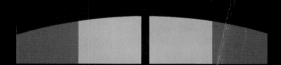

8,25,26,33,34);"Wings" by Robert Cottingham (19,20,27,28,35,36); "Views or Mirrors" by Cary Smith (21,22,29,30,37,38); "Variations on Nature
,4,5,6" by Yoshishige Furakawa (23,24,31,32,39,40)

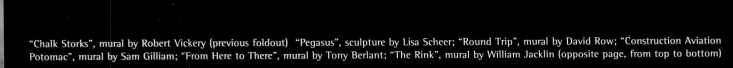

"Chalk Storks", mural by Robert Vickery (previous foldout) "Pegasus", sculpture by Lisa Scheer; "Round Trip", mural by David Row; "Construction Aviation Potomac", mural by Sam Gilliam; "From Here to There", mural by Tony Berlant; "The Rink", mural by William Jacklin (opposite page, from top to bottom)

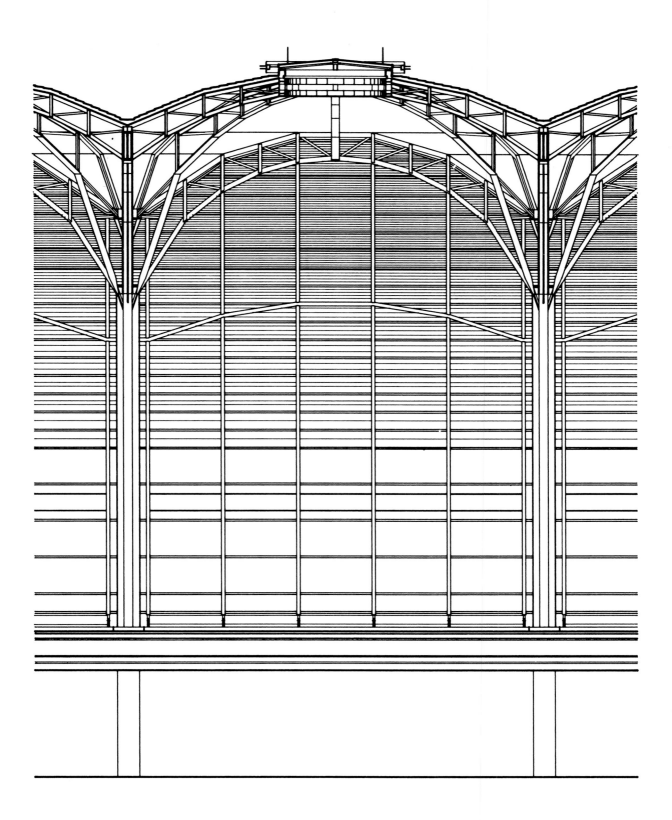

99 100 Al Held laminated and etched glass frieze detail (previous spread) View of airfield from concourse with Jennifer Bartlett's painted fused and laminated glass frieze (left) Section at east wall (above)

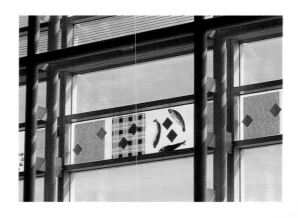

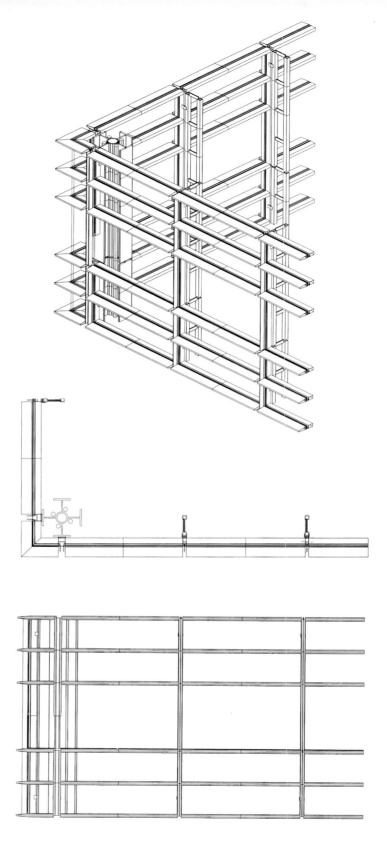

101 102 Architectural Enhancement Program detail photographs of medalions by Frank Stella, Joyce Scott and Sol LeWitt; railing panel by Siah Armajani and glass frieze by Jennifer Bartlett and Al Held (previous spread, from left to right and top to bottom) Corner detail at south end of terminal (top left) View of north outdoor terrace from ticket level (opposite page) Curtain wall elevation, plan and axonometric detail (above)

Project Name: North Terminal, Ronald Reagan
                       Washington National Airport
Owner: Metropolitan Washington Airports
                       Authority, Washington, DC
Location: Washington, DC
Design Architect: Cesar Pelli & Associates

                       1056 Chapel Street
                       New Haven Connecticut 06510
                       203 777 2515 fax 203 787 2856

Honor Award, Community Appearance Alliance of Northern Virginia, 1993
Honor Award, Job of the Year, National Terrazo & Mosaic Association, 1997
Platinum Award, Excellence in Mechanical & Electrical Engineering Support for Buildings, 1998
E.P.R.I. Award, Excellence and Meritorious Contribution to The Art and Science of Lighting, 1998
Honor Award, American Institute of Architects, Connecticut, 1998
Lumen Citation Award, New York Section of the Illuminating Engineering Society, 1998
First Place, Ceilings and Interior Systems Construction Association, 1998
Honor Award, American Institute of Architects, New England, 1999

Design Team, Terminal:	Cesar Pelli, design principal; Fred W. Clarke, project principal; Mark R. Shoemaker, design team leader; Phillip G. Bernstein, project manager; Anthony Markese (rendering on page 50), Barbara Endres, Sharon McGinnis DaSilva, Philip Koether, Isaac Campbell, Lisa Winkelmann, Michael Green (rendeinrg on page 51), Julann Meyers, Philip Nelson, David Toti, Jennifer Carpenter, Sunny Evangelista Carroll, Enrique Pelli-Noble, Alison Horne, Yann Poisson, Bernard Proeschl, Jeanne Smith, James Winkler, Dewitt Zuse, designers.	Associate Architect:	Pierce Goodwin Alexander & Linville, Alexandria, Virginia
		Project Management:	Parsons Management Consultants, Washington, DC
		Structural Engineer:	CBM Engineers Inc., Houston, Texas
		MEP Engineers:	Syska & Hennessy, New York, New York; John J. Christie & Associates, Washington, DC
		Landscape Design:	Balmori Associates Inc., New Haven, Connecticut
		General Contractor:	Site: Hyman/OMNI Building: Morganti McGaughan & Dick Enterprises Joint Venture
Design Team, Parking Garage:	Cesar Pelli, design principal; Fred W. Clarke, project principal; Jeffrey L. Paine, project manager; Rossana Santos, Axel Zemborain, design team leaders; Jerome del Fierro, Timothy Paxton, Fritz Haeg, designers.	Building Area:	1,000,000 square feet
		Date of Design:	1989-1994
Architect of Record:	Leo A. Daly, Washington, DC	Date of Completion:	Summer 1997

Cesar Pelli & Associates, located in New Haven, Connecticut, was established in 1977. Fred Clarke FAIA has been a principal in the firm since 1981 and Rafael Pelli, AIA, since 1993. ❚ Cesar Pelli & Associates is a full service firm of some 80 persons. The firm has worked with corporate, government and private clients to design major public spaces, museums, airports, laboratories, performing arts centers, academic buildings, hotels, office and residential towers, and mixed-use projects. The number of commissions the firm accepts is carefully limited to ensure a high degree of personal involvement by the principals. ❚ The American Institute of Architects awarded Cesar Pelli & Associates its 1989 *Firm Award* in recognition of standard-setting work in architectural design.

Oscar Riera Ojeda is a Boston-based editor and designer who has practiced in the United States, South America and Europe for over fifteen years. Originally from Buenos Aires, he is vice-director of the Spanish-Argentinian magazine *Casas Internacional*, and is the creator of several series of architectural publications for Rockport Publishers in addition to the *Single Building* series, including *Ten Houses, Contemporary World Architects, Architecture in Detail* and *Art and Architecture*. Other architectural publications include Hyper-Realistic Computer Generated Architectural Renderings, the *New American* series (New American House 1 & 2 and New American Apartment) for the Whitney Library of Design, as well as several monographs on the work of renowned architects.

The text was edited by Mark Denton, an architect and writer practicing in Santa Monica, California.

103 104 Dusk shot of landside facade (opposite page) Detail of airside curtain wall (following page)

photographic credits